PIANO · VOCAL · GUITAR
COLDPLAY
SUNRISE

شروق

sunrise

ISBN: 978-1-5400-8218-3

HAL•LEONARD®

Visit Hal Leonard Online at
www.halleonard.com

Contact us:
Hal Leonard
7777 West Bluemound Road
Milwaukee, WI 53213
Email: info@halleonard.com

In Europe, contact:
Hal Leonard Europe Limited
42 Wigmore Street
Marylebone, London, W1U 2RY
Email: info@halleonardeurope.com

In Australia, contact:
Hal Leonard Australia Pty. Ltd.
4 Lentara Court
Cheltenham, Victoria, 3192 Australia
Email: info@halleonard.com.au

شروق

sunrise

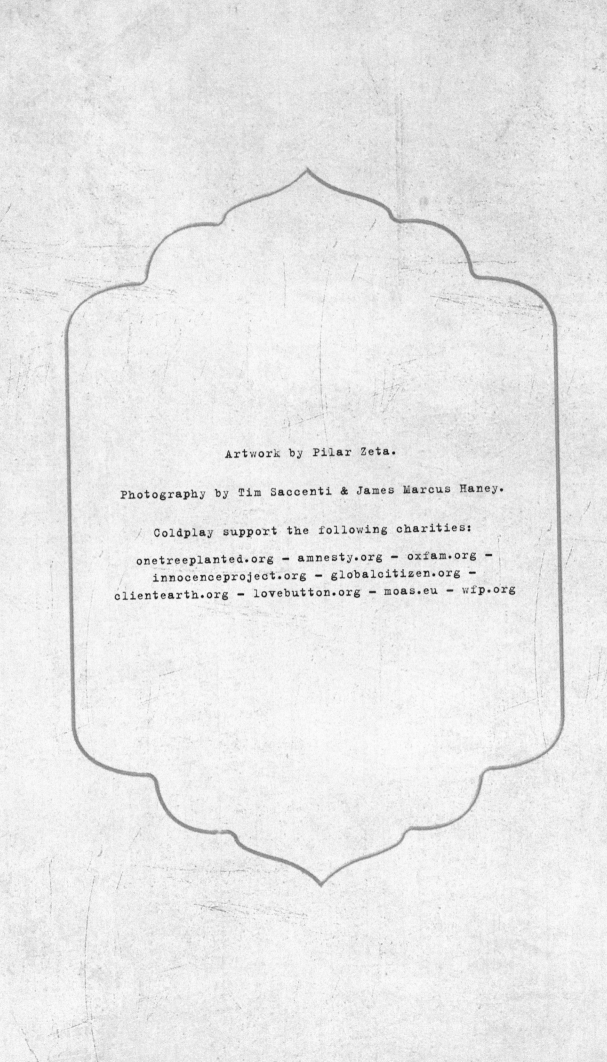

Artwork by Pilar Zeta.

Photography by Tim Saccenti & James Marcus Haney.

Coldplay support the following charities:

onetreeplanted.org – amnesty.org – oxfam.org –
innocenceproject.org – globalcitizen.org –
clientearth.org – lovebutton.org – moas.eu – wfp.org

SUNRISE

Sunrise

Words and Music by Guy Berryman, Jon Buckland,
Will Champion, Chris Martin and Davide Rossi

Church

Words and Music by Guy Berryman, Jon Buckland, Will Champion,
Chris Martin, Jacob Collier, Noura Shakkour, Davide Rossi,
Amjad Sabri, Mikkel Eriksen and Tor Erik Hermansen

Moderately

What can I tell ___ you? When I'm with you, I'm walk-ing on air, ___

watch-ing you sleep - ing there. ___

But what can't I get ___ through? When for ev-'ry-one, ev-'ry-where, ___

you're an-swer-ing ev - 'ry prayer. ___

And when you're rid-ing a wave, _____ oh, won't you ride ___

that wave to me? When you're set-ting your sail _____

oh, can I be _____ your sev-enth sea? When you're rid-ing a wave_

oh, when you're rid-ing a wave._

'Cause when I'm hurt_

then I go to your church._

'Cause when I'm hurt

then I go to your church.

I wor-ship in your church, ba - by, al - ways, ___ I wor-ship in your

church, all the sev - en days ___ I praise and praise.

Trouble In Town

Words and Music by Guy Berryman, Jon Buckland, Will Champion and Chris Martin

- -ter ——— and I get no peace ———
- -ter ——— and I get no peace ———

and I nev - er get ——— re - leased. ———
and I just get more ——— po - lice. ———

And I get no com -

there must be some way.

BrokEn

Words and Music by Guy Berryman, Jon Buckland, Will Champion and Chris Martin

daddy

**Words and Music by Guy Berryman,
Jon Buckland, Will Champion and Chris Martin**

Dad - dy, are you out there? Dad - dy, won't you come and play?

Original recording one semitone higher

28

That's o - kay, —

that's o - kay, I'm o - kay.

To Coda ⊕

Dad - dy, are you out there?

Dad - dy, why'd you run a - way?

Dad - dy, are you o - kay?

Look, Dad, we got the same hair   and, Dad-dy, it's my birth-day.

And all I want to say   is you're

You're so __

WOTW / POTP

Words and Music by Guy Berryman, Jon Buckland, Will Champion and Chris Martin

ARABESQUE

Words and Music by Guy Berryman, Jon Buckland, Will Champion,
Chris Martin, Drew Goddard, Femi Kuti and Paul van Haver

I could be you,— you could be me,— two rain - drops in — the same

sea. You could be me,— I could be you,—

two an - gles of — the same view and we share the same blood.

Comme deux gouttes d'eau —

on se res - semble, __ comme pro - venant de __ la même mère.

(You could be me)   (I could be you)

Comme deux ruis - seaux __   qui se ras - semblent,   pour faire __ les gran - des riv - i -

ères   and we share the same blood.

Yeah, we share the same blood.

Spoken: Music is the weapon,   *music is the weapon of the future.*

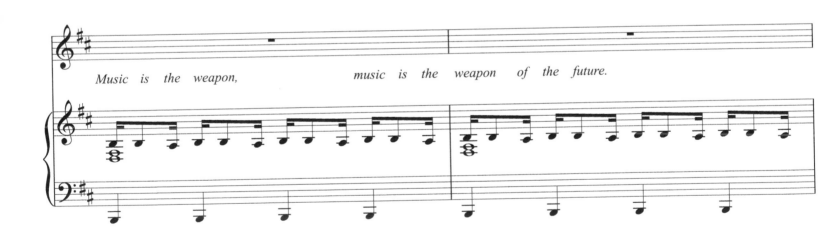

Music is the weapon,   *music is the weapon of the future.*

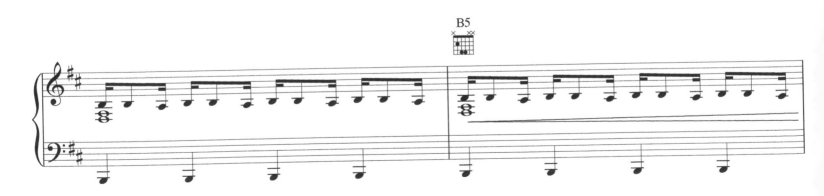

when i need a friend

Words and Music by Guy Berryman, Jon Buckland, Will Champion and Chris Martin

Original recording one semitone lower

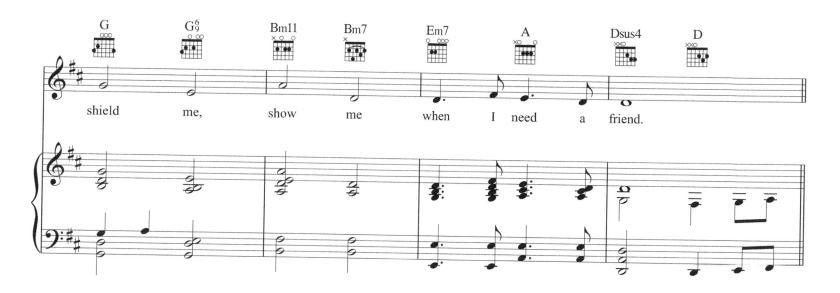

shield me, show me when I need a friend.

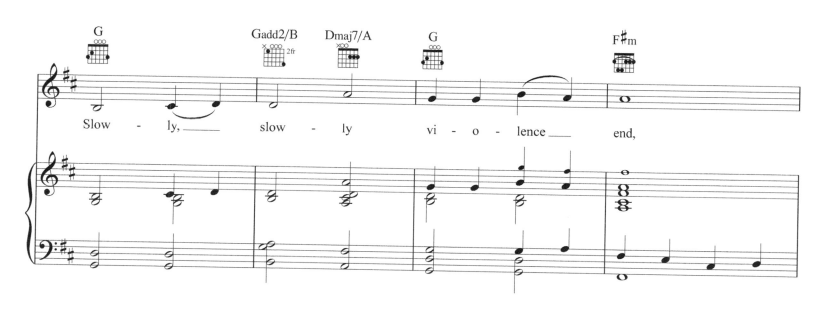

Slow - ly, _____ slow - ly vi - o - lence _____ end,

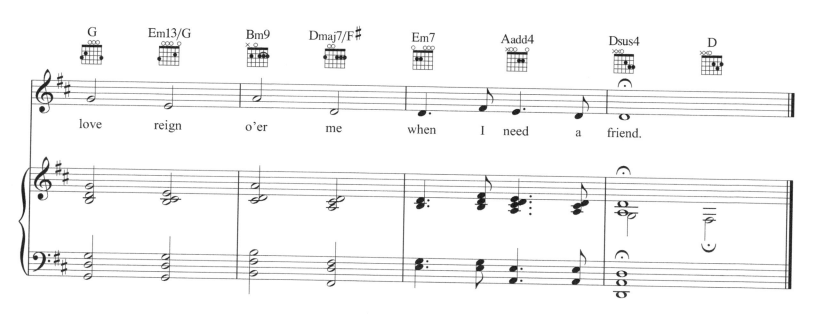

love reign o'er me when I need a friend.

شروق

sunrise

غروب

sunset

please access sunset from
the back of this book

PIANO · VOCAL · GUITAR
COLDPLAY
SUNSET

غروب
sunset

ISBN: 978-1-5400-8218-3

HAL • LEONARD®

Visit Hal Leonard Online at
www.halleonard.com

Contact us:
Hal Leonard
7777 West Bluemound Road
Milwaukee, WI 53213
Email: info@halleonard.com

In Europe, contact:
Hal Leonard Europe Limited
42 Wigmore Street
Marylebone, London, W1U 2RY
Email: info@halleonardeurope.com

In Australia, contact:
Hal Leonard Australia Pty. Ltd.
4 Lentara Court
Cheltenham, Victoria, 3192 Australia
Email: info@halleonard.com.au

SUNSET

GUNS

Words and Music by Guy Berryman, Jon Buckland, Will Champion and Chris Martin

Bb6   F   Bb/D   Bb6   F

cra - zy, { ev-'ry-thing tan - gled__ in blue.__
          ev-'ry-bo - dy but you. _____ }

Bb/D   Bb6   F   F7/Eb

Ev-'ry-one's going fuck-ing cra - zy, may-be I'm _____

Bb   **To Coda** ⊕   F7

__ cra - zy too.

mf

Melt down all the trum-pets, all the trom - bones __ and the drums,

2/4   4/4

8

ORPHANS

Words and Music by Guy Berryman, Jon Buckland,
Will Champion, Chris Martin and Moses Martin

ÈKÓ

Words and Music by Guy Berryman, Jon Buckland, Will Champion and Chris Martin

16

sleep   and say, 'It's al - right,   child.   It's ___ al -

right.'

CRY CRY CRY

Words and Music by Guy Berryman, Jon Buckland, Will Champion,
Chris Martin, Bert Russell, Jerry Ragovoy and Jacob Collier

23

OLD FRIENDS

Words and Music by Guy Berryman, Jon Buckland, Will Champion and Chris Martin

my back, __ once he real-ly saved my life.

Some - times, _ I want to call him __ say, 'Hey, let's

stay up __ 'til morn - ing'. __

And when I close my eyes, when I close my eyes I see you, _____

mf

بنی آدم

Words and Music by Guy Berryman, Jon Buckland, Will Champion,
Chris Martin, Alice Coltrane and Harcourt Whyte

بنی آدم اعضای یک پیکرند

که در آفرینش ز یک گوهرند

چو عضوی به درد آورد روزگار

دگر عضوها را نماند قرار

تو کز محنت دیگران بی غمی

نشاید که نامت نهند آدمی

banī ādam a'zā-ye yekdigar-and
ke dar āfarin-aš ze yek gowhar-and
čo 'ozvī be dard āvarad rūzgār
degar 'ozvhā-rā na-mānad qarār
to k-az mehnat-ē dīgarān bīqam-ī
na-šāyad ke nām-at nahand ādamī

CHAMPION OF THE WORLD

Words and Music by Guy Berryman, Jon Buckland, Will Champion, Chris Martin,
Scott Hutchison, Simon Liddell, Andy Monaghan and Harcourt Whyte

tried my best to be just like the oth-er boys in school.

tried my best to get it right and died in ev-'ry duel. This

mount - tain - side is su - i - cide, _ this dream will nev - er work, _____ still this

sign up - on my head - stone, write: _ 'A cham - pion of the world.' _____

tried my best to stay a-light, __ fly like a fire - work. _____ I

tried my best at tak - ing flight __ but my roc - ket - ship re - versed. _

_____ Oh, re - fer - ee, don't stop the fight, __ ev - 'ry -

one can see I'm hurt. _____ But I'll stand be - fore con -

quis - ta - dors __ till I'm cham - pion of the world _____ (When I

and when I sail, _____ I'm sail - ing __ west.

sail.)

(Know I might fail.) ___ Know-ing I might fail _____ but still I'm hop -

- ing for the best ___ and in my dreams, _

(In my dreams.)

-ing up____ won't work._____ Now I'm rid - ing on____ my rock-

-et ship____ and I'm cham - pion of the world._____

EVERYDAY LIFE

Words and Music by Guy Berryman, Jon Buckland,
Will Champion, Chris Martin and John Metcalfe

What in the world are we go-ing to do? Look at what ev-